1·2
05

READING POWER

Terrell Davis
Super Bowl Running Back
Rob Kirkpatrick

The Rosen Publishing Group's
PowerKids Press ™
New York

1

To the people of Colorado.

Published in 2000 by The Rosen Publishing Group, Inc.
29 East 21st Street, New York, NY 10010

First Edition

Book design: Michael de Guzman

Photo Credits: pp. 5, 9, 13 © Rob Tringali, Jr./SportsChrome USA; p. 7 © Michael Zito/SportsChrome USA; p. 11 © Reuters/Gary Caskey/Archive Photos; p. 15 © Doug Pensinger/Allsport; p. 17 © Rick Stewart/Allsport; p. 19 © Bongarts Photography/SportsChrome

Text Consultant: Linda J. Kirkpatrick, Reading Specialist/Reading Recovery Teacher

Kirkpatrick, Rob.
    Terrell Davis: Super Bowl running back / by Rob Kirkpatrick.
      p. cm. — (Reading power)
    Includes index.
    SUMMARY: Introduces Terrell Davis, star running back for the Denver Broncos.
    ISBN 0-8239-5536-2
    1. Davis, Terrell, 1972– Juvenile literature. 2. Football players—United States Biography Juvenile literature. [1. Davis, Terrell, 1972– 2. Football players. 3. Afro-Americans Biography.]
    I. Title. II. Series
    GV939.D347 K57 1999
    796.332'092—dc21
    [B]   99-16001
                                                  CIP

Manufactured in the United States of America

Contents

Terrell Davis plays football. He is a running back.

5

Terrell plays for the Denver Broncos. He is number 30 on the Broncos.

7

The Broncos like to get the ball to Terrell. Terrell is very fast. He is good at running with the ball.

Terrell can catch the ball, too.

11

Terrell gets a lot of touchdowns. When he gets a touchdown, Terrell salutes the players on his team.

13

Terrell played football in school. He played for the Georgia Bulldogs. He had number 33 on his shirt.

15

Terrell played in Super Bowl 32. He ran with the ball a lot.

Terrell scored three touchdowns in Super Bowl 32. He helped the Broncos win.

19

Terrell got to play in Super Bowl 33. He got to run with the ball.

Terrell talks into a mike. He tells people about the game.

Here are more books to read about
Terrell Davis and football:

Terrell Davis
by Jeff Savage
Lerner Publications (1999)

Football Stars (All Aboard Reading)
by Jim Campbell, illustrated by
Sydelle A. Kramer
Grosset & Dunlap (1997)

Due to the changing nature of Internet links,
PowerKids Press has developed an online list of
Web sites related to the subject of this book.
This site is updated regularly. Please use this link
to access the list:
www.powerkidslinks.com/reapow/tedav/

Glossary

game (GAYM) When two teams play football.

running back (RUHN-ing BAK) The player who runs with the ball.

salute (suh-LOOT) To raise your hand to your forehead as a symbol of respect.

Super Bowl (SOO-per BOHL) A game that the two best football teams play at the end of the year.

touchdown (TUCH-down) When a player carries the ball into the end zone and scores six points for his team.

Index

Word Count: 137

Note to Librarians, Teachers, and Parents

　　If reading is a challenge, Reading Power is a solution! Reading Power is perfect for readers who want high-interest subject matter at an accessible reading level. These fact-filled, photo-illustrated books are designed for readers who want straightforward vocabulary, engaging topics, and a manageable reading experience. With clear picture/text correspondence, leveled Reading Power books put the reader in charge. Now readers have the power to get the information they want and the skills they need in a user-friendly format.